OPPOSING VIEWPOINTS RESOURCE CENTER

Critical Thinking Skills Booklet

THOMSON

GALE

Detroit • New York • San Francisco • New Haven, Conn. • Waterville, Maine • London

THOMSON

GALE

**Opposing Viewpoints Resource Center:
Critical Thinking Skills Booklet**

Library of Congress Control Number: 2007929083

ISBN 978-1-4144-4424-6
Contact your Thomson Gale sales representative for ordering information

Printed in the United States of America
10 9 8 7 6 5 4 3 2 1

Table of Contents

To the Teacher iv
Lesson Guide v

Skill 1
What does it mean? 1
Let's try it! A simple example 2
An example using an actual passage ... 3
Now you try it 4

Skill 2
What does it mean? 5
Let's try it! A simple example 6
An example using an actual passage 7
Now you try it 8

Skill 3
What does it mean? 9
Let's try it! A simple example 10
An example using an actual passage ... 11
Now you try it 12

Skill 4
What does it mean? 13
Let's try it! A simple example 14
An example using an actual passage ... 15
Now you try it 16

Skill 5
What does it mean? 17
Let's try it! A simple example 18
An example using an actual passage ... 19
Now you try it 20

Skill 6
What does it mean? 21
Let's try it! A simple example 22
An example using an actual passage ... 23
Now you try it 24

Skill 7
What does it mean? 25
Let's try it! A simple example 26
An example using an actual passage ... 27
Now you try it 28

Skill 8
What does it mean? 29
Let's try it! A simple example 30
An example using an actual passage ... 31
Now you try it 32

Skill 9
What does it mean? 33
Let's try it! A simple example 34
An example using an actual passage ... 35
Now you try it 36

Skill 10
What does it mean? 37
Let's try it! A simple example 38
An example using an actual passage ... 39
Now you try it 40

Skill 11
What does it mean? 41
Let's try it! A simple example 42
An example using an actual passage ... 43
Now you try it 44

Skill 12
What does it mean? 45
Let's try it! A simple example 46
An example using an actual passage ... 47
Now you try it 48

Skill 13
What does it mean? 49
Let's try it! A simple example 50
An example using an actual passage ... 51
Now you try it 52

Skill 14
What does it mean? 53
Let's try it! A simple example 54
An example using an actual passage ... 55
Now you try it 56

Skill 15
What does it mean? 57
Let's try it! A simple example 58
An example using an actual passage ... 59
Now you try it 60

Skill 16
What does it mean? 61
Let's try it! A simple example 62
An example using an actual passage ... 63
Now you try it 64

Skill 17
What does it mean? 65
Let's try it! A simple example 66
An example using an actual passage ... 67
Now you try it 68

Skill 18
What does it mean? 69
Let's try it! A simple example 70
An example using an actual passage ... 71
Now you try it 72

Answer Pages
Skill 1 answer page 73
Skill 1 answer page 74
Skill 2 answer page 75
Skill 2 answer page 76
Skill 3 answer page 77
Skill 3 answer page 78
Skill 4 answer page 79
Skill 4 answer page 80
Skill 5 answer page 81
Skill 5 answer page 82
Skill 6 answer page 83
Skill 6 answer page 84
Skill 7 answer page 85
Skill 7 answer page 86
Skill 8 answer page 87
Skill 8 answer page 88
Skill 9 answer page 89
Skill 9 answer page 90
Skill 10 answer page 91
Skill 10 answer page 92
Skill 11 answer page 93
Skill 11 answer page 94
Skill 12 answer page 95
Skill 12 answer page 96
Skill 13 answer page 97
Skill 13 answer page 98
Skill 14 answer page 99
Skill 14 answer page 100
Skill 15 answer page 101
Skill 15 answer page 102
Skill 16 answer page 103
Skill 16 answer page 104
Skill 17 answer page 105
Skill 17 answer page 106
Skill 18 answer page 107
Skill 18 answer page 108

To the Teacher:

Thomson Gale reviewed various critical thinking approaches to compile a list of 18 critical thinking skills. The lessons in this Guide will help you and your students define and focus on these skills. Students will naturally engage in critical thinking and apply the skills as they read articles and complete activities in Opposing Viewpoints Resource Center: Critical Thinking.

These 18 skills are broken into five higher-level skills:

❶ Locating Credible, Relevant Information

❷ Evaluating Sources of Information

❸ Comprehending Information

❹ Analyzing Information

❺ Synthesizing and Applying Information

OVRC: Critical Thinking provides students with challenging activities and assessments that are built around content that aligns to state curriculum standards and library programs. Features like "Questions to Think About," "Words to Know," and "Find Out More" encourage interaction, problem-solving, and critical thinking. Each of the 250 topics has three readings to foster balanced, unbiased research: an overview and two viewpoint essays.

OVRC is based on the acclaimed print series Opposing Viewpoints by Greenhaven Press, an imprint of Thomson Gale. Since its release, OVRC has received wide acclaim for its ease of use, depth and breadth of content, and focus on current issues.

Critical thinking is inherent in OVRC. Teachers told us that they needed more focus on critical thinking skills because of increased emphasis on these skills in state-mandated testing and 21st Century Workforce Skills, so we are happy to provide it.

Welcome to Opposing Viewpoints Resource Center:
Critical Thinking Skills Lessons!

Teaching Critical Thinking Skills

Lesson Guide

The Opposing Viewpoints Resource Center: Critical Thinking provides a powerful tool to help your students develop and practice critical thinking skills. The 18 lessons in this book will help you support your students in the development of their critical thinking skills by describing in detail what the skills are and how to apply them and by providing targeted practice for each of the skills.

The lessons are designed to support both students who may be struggling with applying critical thinking skills in OVRC: Critical Thinking and those who want to improve their critical thinking skills. These lessons will help students transfer these skills to all classes and, most important, into everyday life. Each lesson may be copied in part or in whole as handouts for your students.

In the development of OVRC: Critical Thinking, Thomson Gale worked with a diverse group of educators to examine 21st Century Skills, information literacy skills, and critical thinking skills. Their research led to this list of 18 critical thinking skills, the focus of the OVRC: Critical Thinking content.

The "Questions to Think About" ask students to bring previous knowledge on the topic into discussion. "Words to Know" focuses on words that help learners identify points of view and their legitimacy. Each question in "Take the Test" focuses on one of the 18 critical thinking skills. Finally, "Find Out More" asks students to combine multiple skills and express an opinion on a topic after finding and evaluating sources within OVRC: Critical Thinking.

Here is a brief explanation of each of the 18 critical thinking skills:

Locating Credible, Relevant Information

1. **Evaluating the credibility of information sources**
   - Find sources of information that can be relied on to be accurate, trustworthy, and authoritative

2. **Distinguishing relevant from irrelevant facts**
   - Examine sources of information to determine their usefulness for a specific question or topic

Evaluating Sources of Information

3. **Distinguishing fact from opinion**
- Evaluate a statement to determine if the statement is a personal judgment

4. **Recognizing contradictions**
- Identify conclusions that are inconsistent or disagree with cited facts and events

5. **Recognizing bias**
- Identify unfair preferences, prejudices, prejudgments, or dislikes

 Comprehending Information

6. **Clarifying issues, conclusions, or beliefs**
- Explain ideas and statements to make them clearer

7. **Developing criteria for evaluation: clarifying values and standards**
- Identify factors that are used to make decisions and judgments

8. **Analyzing arguments, interpretations, beliefs, or theories**
- Examine and investigate ideas in greater detail

9. **Identifying assumptions**
- Recognize ideas, beliefs, and theories that are not stated by an author

10. **Making plausible inferences, predictions, or interpretations**
- Provide a reasonable explanation, forecast, or conclusion from information

 Analyzing Information

11. **Analyzing or evaluating actions or policies**
- Examine the consequence of an undertaking or plan in great detail

12. **Comparing analogous situations: transferring insights to new contexts**
- Recognize the similarity between two events; use knowledge of one event to understand another event

13. **Recognizing cause and effect**
- Identify how one event makes another event happen

 Synthesizing and Applying Information

14. **Demonstrating reasoned judgment**
- Show that an opinion or conclusion is based on evidence and logic

15. **Identifying alternatives**
- List different possible conclusions, courses of action, or beliefs to choose between

16. Exploring implications and consequences
- Identify the possible effects of different courses of action

17. Generating or assessing solutions
- Develop answers and explanations for problems

18. Drawing and testing conclusions
- Reconsider a decision based on an analysis of its effects and consequences

Lesson Structure

Each of the skills lessons follows the same sequence of steps. Each lesson includes three exercises of increasing difficulty. The exercises can be copied and provided to students. Answers to the exercises are located in the back of the book.

What does it mean? provides an explanation of the skill by introducing a student-friendly scenario that demonstrates the skill or provides an opportunity to exercise the skill in a familiar situation. The scenario is followed by a careful description of the skill and suggestions for techniques or ways of thinking that help the student use the skill. These techniques are built into the questions students are asked in the later exercises.

Why is it important? provides rationales for knowing how to use the skill. These rationales focus on the real-world, rather than academic, value of the critical thinking skill.

Let's try it! A simple example uses the student-friendly example introduced at the beginning of the lesson to work through an application of the critical thinking skill. Students are asked to provide answers to questions that guide them through the application of the skill. Answers and explanations are in the answers section at the end of the book.

Let's try it! An example using an actual passage uses an excerpt from one of the articles in the OVRC as a basis for practicing the critical thinking skill. Students are asked to provide answers to questions that guide them through the application of the skill with this more difficult example. The questions for this example parallel the questions for the simpler example. Answers and explanations are found in the answers section at the end of the book.

Now you try it! directs the student to locate an article in the OVRC and use that article as the basis for applying the critical thinking skill by answering questions in the exercise. These questions do not have answers provided, and you may wish to use students' responses to this exercise as teaching tools to demonstrate to the class how to apply this critical thinking skill to the articles in the OVRC.

Focus on Critical Thinking Skills

Skill 1

Evaluating the credibility of information sources

• Find sources of information that can be relied on to be accurate, trustworthy, and authoritative.

What does it mean?

> Pedro had been working out at the gym for several weeks. He wanted to build his muscle mass, but no matter how much he exercised his muscles seemed to stay the same size. Pedro's friend Tim suggested that Pedro try a protein powder called *Muscle X*. Tim said that his trainer had first given it to him and he could already tell the difference. Pedro read the information on the *Muscle X* bottle. The bottle's label said the powder was scientifically formulated to build muscles.

When anyone learns a new piece of information, he or she must decide whether the source of that information is reliable or credible. **A credible information source is one that you can trust to give you correct information** about a certain topic. When you evaluate the credibility of a source, you should ask two questions: who is presenting the information, and what are that source's interests? Knowing the source of the claim lets you evaluate the source's expertise on the subject. For example, most claims about medical information should be trusted only if they come from a doctor or other trained medical personnel. If the source presenting the information seems to have expertise, next consider whether the source has anything to gain from your believing the information. For example, if the information comes from a scientific institution, you may want to consider where the institution's funding comes from. Some institutions are funded by corporations that stand to profit from certain scientific claims. This may cause the institution to present information in a manner that is partial to the corporation's services or products.

Why is it important?

Knowing whether a source of information is credible will help you evaluate the validity of any claims you hear or read. This will help you identify trustworthy information that can then be used to help you make the best possible decisions

Let's try it!

A simple example

> Pedro had been working out at the gym for several weeks. He wanted to build his muscle mass, but no matter how much he exercised his muscles seemed to stay the same size. Pedro's friend Tim suggested that Pedro try a protein powder called *Muscle X*. Tim said that his trainer had first given it to him and he could already tell the difference. Pedro read the information on the *Muscle X* bottle. The bottle's label said the powder was scientifically formulated to build muscles.

What are the sources for the information Pedro received about *Muscle X*?

_____

_____

Could you consider any of these sources to be experts on the subject matter?

_____

_____

_____

What might any of the sources have to gain by supplying Pedro with the information about *Muscle X*?

_____

_____

_____

Based on what you know, would you consider any of the sources to be credible? If not, who might be a credible source of information about *Muscle X*?

_____

_____

Let's try it!

An example using an actual passage

> The American Medical Association (AMA) appreciates the opportunity to submit this statement to the Senate Commerce Committee for the record on the important issue of "violence in the media." . . . The sad fact is that, over the course of time, violence has been imperceptibly woven into the fabric of our nation and permeates every aspect of our daily lives, including many of our sources of entertainment. The general public intuitively understands this; in a national poll, 79% of Americans indicated that they believed that violence in the media directly contributes to the problem of actual violence in our society. The AMA believes that violence, including "virtual violence," has become a major medical and public health epidemic.

Identify the source of the information in this paragraph.

_____

Do you think this is a credible source for information about public health? Explain.

_____

_____

Do you think this is a credible source for information about the media? Explain.

_____

_____

The paragraph includes information about a national poll of the opinions of the American public. How would you evaluate the credibility of their stance on violence in the media?

_____

_____

_____

Now you try it!

Use one of the articles from the topic "Alcoholism" (article document numbers EJ3010217132, EJ3010217249, and EJ3010238240), or choose your own article from the Opposing Viewpoints Resource Center that takes a position on an issue. Identify the sources of the information in the article and whether you think these sources are credible.

Article Title: _____

Article Document Number: _____

Identify the sources of the information:

_____

_____

_____

_____

_____

_____

_____

_____

Explain why the sources are or are not credible:

_____

_____

_____

_____

_____

_____

Focus on Critical Thinking Skills

Skill 2 — Distinguishing relevant from irrelevant facts

• Examine sources of information to determine their usefulness for a specific question or topic.

What does it mean?

Gina is writing a report on what causes the seasons. She looks up the word *season* in the index of a textbook. The index leads her to the following two passages:

❏ As we move around the Sun over the course of the year, we see different parts of the Milky Way galaxy in the night sky. This is why the constellations, or star patterns, seem to change in seasonal cycles.

❏ When light rays strike the Northern Hemisphere most directly, the season of summer occurs. When light rays strike the Northern Hemisphere at an angle, the season of winter occurs.

When you are analyzing a problem, you need to determine what facts are relevant to that problem. **Something that is relevant has bearing on the matter at hand.** Judging relevancy can be difficult and is often a matter of opinion. To determine a fact's relevancy, you must first start by identifying the issue under consideration. This first step is necessary because a fact can be relevant or irrelevant only in relation to a specific topic. Next, ask yourself how the fact relates to the issue. Is the fact directly related? Would the fact add to a person's knowledge about that particular issue? If so, the fact is relevant to the issue. If not, the fact is most likely irrelevant to the issue.

Why is it important?

When you draw conclusions about an issue, you should consider only relevant facts. Considering only relevant facts helps ensure that your conclusions are based on a logical and reasonable analysis of the available information.

Let's try it!

A simple example

> Gina is writing a report on what causes the seasons. She looks up the
> word *season* in the index of a textbook. The index leads her to the fol-
> lowing two passages:
>
> ❑ As we move around the Sun over the course of the year, we see
> different parts of the Milky Way galaxy in the night sky. This is
> why the constellations, or star patterns, seem to change in sea-
> sonal cycles.
>
> ❑ When light rays strike the Northern Hemisphere most directly,
> the season of summer occurs. When light rays strike the Northern
> Hemisphere at an angle, the season of winter occurs.

What is the topic of Gina's report?

_____

Are either of the two passages Gina found in the textbook relevant to the topic she is
researching? Explain.

_____

_____

_____

Are either of the two passages Gina found in the textbook irrelevant to the topic she is
researching? Explain.

_____

_____

_____

_____

Let's try it!

An example using an actual passage

> The heart-wrenching spectacle of teeming masses hazarding fearsome hardships in order to leave Mexico speaks in condemnation of the policies of Mexico's government, not ours. Mexico's wealth remains concentrated among very, very few. Its government has consistently refused to undertake massive efforts to achieve a more equitable distribution of that nation's wealth. Given these facts, and given further Mexico's richness in natural resources, it is Mexico's president, Vicente Fox, and his predecessors who are clearly the true villains in the lives of desperate Mexicans who understandably seek to escape to California or elsewhere in the United States. President Fox is cynical and irresponsible when he chastises the United States for not accepting an ever-increasing number of his own nationals, for whom his government has so miserably failed to provide.

Suppose you were researching the topic of illegal immigration. Would the information in the above passage be relevant? Explain.

_____

_____

_____

_____

Suppose you were researching the topic of poverty in the United States. Would the information in the above passage be relevant? Explain.

_____

_____

_____

_____

Now you try it!

Use one of the articles from the topic "Marijuana" (article document numbers EJ3010381206 and EJ3010381207). These articles discuss evidence of the effects of marijuana on users. Identify any information in the articles that is relevant only to the direct effect of marijuana on a person's physical health. Identify five pieces of information that would not be relevant to this topic.

Article Title: _____

Article Document Number: _____

Information of direct relevance to physical health:

_____

_____

_____

Five pieces of information not relevant to physical health:

_____

_____

_____

_____

_____

_____

Focus on Critical Thinking Skills

Skill 3   Distinguishing fact from opinion

- Evaluate a statement to determine if the statement is a personal judgment.

What does it mean?

> Lee went camping at a state park near his home. A ranger at the park's visitor center told Lee that the park contained three different ecosystems and had some of the most diverse animal life in the country. The ranger also explained that the park was more scenic than other nearby state parks because of the park's many waterfalls. The ranger ended her talk by pointing out the park's most challenging hiking trails on a map and telling Lee about the different plants and animals that he was likely to see on each trail.

Much of the information you come across in magazines, books, and the news is a mixture of facts and opinions. **Facts are statements that can be proven or disproven by objective data. Opinions are statements that express a judgment, view, conclusion, or interpretation.** Unlike facts, opinions cannot be proven to be true or false. To determine whether a statement is a fact or an opinion, you can ask yourself whether there is, or could be, objective information that could prove the statement true or false. If such information exists, then the statement is a fact, not an opinion. For example, the statement that an oak is a tree can be considered a fact because the characteristics of the physical object can be compared with the list of characteristics of a tree. The statement that an oak is beautiful is an opinion because no evidence can be produced that proves, or disproves, that oaks are beautiful.

Why is it important?

When you are able to distinguish fact from opinion, you will be able to identify statements that are only interpretations of an event or object. And you will know that there may be other interpretations of that same event or object that could be just as valid.

Let's try it!

A simple example

Lee went camping at a state park near his home. A ranger at the park's visitor center told Lee that the park contained three different ecosystems and had some of the most diverse animal life in the country. The ranger also explained that the park was more scenic than other nearby state parks because of the park's many waterfalls. The ranger ended her talk by pointing out the park's most challenging hiking trails on a map and telling Lee about the different plants and animals that he was likely to see on each trail.

List all of the facts that Lee learned from the park ranger.

_____

_____

_____

_____

List all of the opinions that Lee heard from the park ranger.

_____

_____

_____

_____

Let's try it!

An example using an actual passage

> The buzz was everything a restaurateur could ask for when the high-end Chicago sushi restaurant *Heat* opened. . . . "Fresh" was the word on everyone's lips and soon the restaurant was packed with people clambering to taste the creations of chef-owner Kee Chan and his staff. Then the letters and phone calls started. Unfortunately for Chan, those weren't from fans. News of *Heat's* fresh sashimi had reached animal rights activists, and several of the restaurant's dishes were a bit too fresh for them. . . . Fish arrived at the table fully alive—with chunks cut out of the belly. . . . Chan says he tried to explain to the activists who approached him that it's a common practice in Japan to serve live fish. . . . Chan's arguments fell on deaf—or disgusted—ears. The Bureau of Animal Welfare ordered *Heat* to stop what [it was] doing, and [the restaurant] complied. . . . Saying that chopping the heads off aquatic creatures behind the scenes hasn't hurt his business—or the freshness of the fish, Chan concludes, "We live in the United States and we have to make everybody happy."

List five facts given by the author in the passage.

_____

_____

_____

_____

_____

List five opinions given by the author in the passage.

_____

_____

_____

_____

_____

Now you try it!

Use one of the articles from the topic "Women Soldiers" (article document numbers EJ3010320101, EJ3010320207, and EJ3010320206), or choose your own article from the Opposing Viewpoints Resource Center that takes a position on an issue. Distinguish between statements of fact and statements of opinion in the article.

Article Title: _____

Article Document Number: _____

Identify ten facts stated in the article: _____

_____

_____

_____

_____

_____

_____

Identify ten opinions stated in the article: _____

_____

_____

_____

_____

_____

_____

Focus on Critical Thinking Skills

Skill 4 — Recognizing contradictions

• Identify conclusions that are inconsistent or disagree with cited facts and events.

What does it mean?

> You read in the newspaper that your town's city council has approved the construction of three new roads around your town. All three of the roads will be tolled (drivers will be charged a fee to use them). The mayor explains that the council came to the decision because tolling drivers on the new roads is the fastest way to pay for their construction. The mayor also assured the citizens that as soon as the construction costs of the new roads were paid for, the tollbooths would be removed. The article ended by stating that in addition to the toll booths on the new roads, permanent toll booths also would be added to another local highway that had been constructed 10 years ago.

Sometimes a statement or conclusion is inconsistent with known facts or a previous statement. Thus, the statement or conclusion contradicts, or disagrees with, the other information. Generally, this means that **either the facts or the contradictory statement is incorrect.** Sometimes contradictions are easy to recognize. For example, suppose a politician votes for a bill to increase property taxes but later states that he does not support any type of tax increase. In this case, the politician's actions contradicted his words. Other contradictions may be harder to recognize. To identify hidden contradictions, you may have to follow every step of a person's train of thought until you come across a break in logic.

Why is it important?

The ability to recognize contradictions is a cornerstone of critical thinking. This skill will allow you to analyze another person's argument for correct and consistent logic. This skill also will allow you to focus on the contradictions between two opposing arguments, so that you can pinpoint the root of their conflicting views.

Let's try it!

A simple example

> You read in the newspaper that your town's city council has approved the construction of three new roads around your town. All three of the roads will be tolled (drivers will be charged a fee to use them). The mayor explains that the council came to the decision because tolling drivers on the new roads is the fastest way to pay for their construction. The mayor also assured the citizens that as soon as the construction costs of the new roads were paid for, the tollbooths would be removed. The article ended by stating that in addition to the toll booths on the new roads, permanent toll booths also would be added to another local highway that had been constructed 10 years ago.

Are there any contradictions in the newspaper article about toll roads? Start by identifying any facts, interpretations, or opinions given in the article. Next, look for any inconsistencies between the facts, interpretations, and opinions. How do the facts, interpretations, or opinions compare? Are there any contradictions between any of these statements?

What are some facts, interpretations, or opinions presented in the article?

_____

_____

_____

_____

_____

Are there contradictions between any of the statements in the article? Explain.

_____

_____

_____

_____

Let's try it!

An example using an actual passage

> In recent years, scholars and intellectuals have insisted that Islam is a religion that has been taken over by fundamentalist extremists, who pose a threat to American security. There is no such thing as Islamic "fundamentalism," however, because the teachings of the Koran are infallible and cannot be bent and shaped to fit modern times or fads. People of the Islamic faith have the right and duty to practice their beliefs as they have for more than thirteen hundred years. While Islam may seem fundamentalist to Westerners who sanction all forms of decadent sexual and social behavior, the teaching of Muhammad cannot be changed to please those of other faiths who would rather that Muslims behaved and believed as they do. It is unacceptable to smear the religious beliefs of Muslims with the negative term "fundamentalism" because the tenets of the faith must remain as Muhammad dictated them in the seventh century.

Recognizing contradictions in actual passages can be difficult. The word *fundamentalism* is defined as an "adherence to a belief" or a "point of view characterized by rigid adherence to fundamental or basic principles." Given the definition of *fundamentalism* and the information presented in the passage, do you think the author makes any contradictory statements about fundamentalism in Islam? Explain

_____

_____

_____

_____

_____

_____

_____

_____

_____

Now you try it!

Choose one of the articles from the topic "Homosexuality" (article document numbers EJ3010143239 and EJ3010359101), or choose your own article from the Opposing Viewpoints Resource Center that takes a position on an issue. Identify at least one contradictory statement made in the article. You may wish to begin by identifying all of the conclusions mentioned in the article. Then, follow the logic the author uses to reach each of the conclusions and look for inconsistencies or statements that contradict the conclusion.

Article Title: _____

Article Document Number: _____

Write down a conclusion or statement from the article and the contradictory statement:

_____

_____

_____

_____

_____

_____

_____

_____

_____

_____

Focus on Critical Thinking Skills

Skill 5   Recognizing bias

- Identify unfair preferences, prejudices, prejudgments, or dislikes.

What does it mean?

> You have come down with a cold and want to buy medicine to help relieve your symptoms. At the pharmacy, you see a cold medication that states on the label that it is the most powerful over-the-counter cold medicine available. The label also says the medicine is FDA approved and doctor-recommended. Underneath the name of the medicine, the label states, "Get rid of your cold in less than 4 hours!"

Much of the information that you come across daily is communicated in a biased way. **A bias is a viewpoint or belief that causes a person to be unable to make an objective judgment.** A person who has a bias may distort information to support his or her interests. Because bias is so common, it is important that you evaluate any claims presented to you before you accept them as the truth. The following questions will help you determine whether a statement contains bias:

Who made the statement?

What does that person have to gain by your believing the statement?

Is there evidence to support the claims made in the statement?

Does the statement make sense?

Why is it important?

Once you have started evaluating statements for bias, you will quickly see that a large part of the information you encounter is presented in a biased manner. Biased information is used to sell products and promote certain belief systems. If you can recognize bias, you can judge the statements in an impartial manner. This will help you to make decisions with outcomes that match your goals.

Let's try it!

A simple example

> You have come down with a cold and want to buy medicine to help relieve your symptoms. At the pharmacy, you see a cold medication that states on the label that it is the most powerful over-the-counter cold medicine available. The label also says the medicine is FDA approved and doctor-recommended. Underneath the name of the medicine, the label states, "Get rid of your cold in less than 4 hours!"

Does the information on the cold-medicine label come from an unbiased source? Explain.

_____

_____

_____

Does any of the information on the cold-medicine label appear to be trustworthy? If so, which piece(s) of information?

_____

_____

_____

Does any of the information appear to go against common sense? If so, which piece(s) of information?

_____

_____

What person do you think could provide unbiased information about the medicine?

_____

_____

_____

Let's try it!

An example using an actual passage

> The abortion license has helped to erode the moral foundations of the American civic community. Right now we are not the country we ought to be. That is why our national conscience is troubled. That distress is, to us, a sign of moral vitality. We speak now because we seek to defend the America we love. We speak to promote the cause of an America in which women and men, together, rebuild the fabric of civil society by acknowledging our common responsibility to serve and protect the weakest and most vulnerable among us. We speak for a rebirth of freedom in these United States: a freedom that finds its fulfillment in goodness.

Is the author of this passage pro- or anti-abortion? Explain.

_____

_____

_____

_____

_____

If the next paragraph gave information about abortion statistics, would you expect the information to be biased? If so, what sort of bias would the information have?

_____

_____

_____

_____

_____

Now you try it!

Compare two of the articles from the topic "Hunting" (article document numbers EJ3010088225 and EJ3010088226), or choose your own articles from the Opposing Viewpoints Resource Center that take a position on an issue. Look for instances of bias in the articles.

Article Title: _____

Article Document Number: _____

Write down statements from either of the articles that seem to contain bias:

_____

_____

_____

_____

_____

_____

_____

_____

_____

_____

_____

_____

_____

_____

Focus on Critical Thinking Skills

Skill 6   Clarifying issues, conclusions, or beliefs

• Explain ideas and statements to make them clearer

What does it mean?

> The swim team is having a meeting. They haven't won at a swim meet in three weeks. "Right now we practice 10 hours each week. I move that we step that up to 20 hours each week," says Bryce. "If we were practicing more, we'd be performing better. Double our practice time and there's no way we're not going to be better prepared for next week's meet."

It is possible that the very first step in any critical thinking exercise is to clarify exactly what is before you. This may be a set of circumstances, someone's conclusions, or someone's beliefs. This means that each person should understand an issue and that everybody should understand it in the same way. Faced with a situation—the swim team's bad performance at meets—the team has to try to understand what the real cause is. There is no sense working on solutions to a problem until you know what the problem really is. Bryce has decided that the problem is lack of technical skill. Therefore, his solution is to increase practice time so they can work on those skills. Notice that Bryce began by stating his solution to the problem. To clarify the problem, the first step probably should be for the team to come to a common understanding of the cause of the poor performance. The team could spend a lot of time arguing about whether they want to double their practice hours. But they would be better off spending some time determining whether lack of technical skill is really the cause of their poor performance.

Why is it important?

Clarifying issues is a key part of critical thinking. How many times have you been in the middle of an argument when the other person says, "That's what I was saying!" The argument dissolves because, as it turned out, you both thought the same thing. For any argument or problem-solving situation to be productive, the issues, conclusions, and beliefs involved in it must be clear to everybody involved.

Let's try it!

A simple example

> The swim team is having a meeting. They haven't won at a swim meet in three weeks. "Right now we practice 10 hours each week. I move that we step that up to 20 hours each week," says Bryce. "If we were practicing more, we'd be performing better. Double our practice time and there's no way we're not going to be better prepared for next week's meet."

Bryce's assumption represents only one of many possible causes for the team's performance. Suggest at least two other possibilities, using a clear explanation

_____

_____

_____

_____

_____

_____

_____

_____

_____

_____

_____

_____

_____

_____

_____

Let's try it!

An example using an actual passage

> "During a six-year period from 1985 to 1991, the rate of homicide committed by 13- and 14-year-old boys was up 157 percent; the rate of homicide committed by 15-year-old boys was up 212 percent," said Jack Levin, director of the program for the study of violence and conflict at Northeastern University. "These statistics tell us that something's wrong."

Begin by restating the speaker's conclusion in clearer terms. What specifically is he saying is happening? Then list the statistics the speaker uses to support it.

Restate the speaker's conclusion:

_____

_____

_____

His statistical proofs are:

_____

_____

Think about the speaker's statistical argument. Is there a way these statistics could be made clearer, or could they be presented in a different way?

_____

_____

_____

_____

_____

Now you try it!

Use one of the articles from the topic "Obesity" (article document numbers EJ3010380214 and EJ3010380215), or choose your own article from the Opposing Viewpoints Resource Center that takes a position on an issue. Identify a portion of the article in which the author is not being clear in an argument or presentation of information.

Article Title: _____

Article Document Number: _____

Restate the author's conclusion:

_____

_____

_____

Restate the author's arguments:

_____

_____

Think about the speaker's argument. Is there a way the argument could be made clearer or presented differently?

_____

_____

_____

_____

_____

Focus on Critical Thinking Skills

Skill 7 | ## Developing criteria for evaluation: clarifying values and standards

• Identify factors that are used to make decisions and judgments

What does it mean?

A grade school in North Dakota announced it was cancelling recess in the winter months, from November through February. "We have so much snow and such cold temperatures during those months, we can't let the kids outside anyway," said the principal. The school board approved this move, saying the school could use the time to prepare students for tests.

We make decisions all the time. We come to our decisions by making judgments. This means we use what we know about a situation plus certain judgment criteria to decide on an action. But two people can look at the same situation, make different judgments about it, and come to different decisions. How can this be? Behind the judgments are people's values and standards. Suppose three people have to decide whether to let students play outside on a day with freezing temperatures. Person A thinks students need to be toughened up, so she decides to let the students go out. Person B hates winter, so he decides to keep the students in. And Person C thinks recess is a waste of school time, so she decides to keep the students in. Each person looks at the same situation, but his or her values lead to different decisions. Even B and C, who come to the same decision, base that decision on different values. Decisions also can be made on the basis of whether the outcomes will meet certain standards. It may be that Person A has been involved in programs to increase physical fitness of students. The decision to keep recess meets her standard that a decision improve the fitness of students. Person B may be concerned about declining academic achievement. The decision to cancel recess meets her standard that a decision should benefit academic performance.

Why is it important?

Learning to clarify the values and standards people use to come to decisions is important because it helps you understand why people make decisions. Rather than argue about which decision is right, which is often a dead-end, you can try to get people to see how a decision might change given different values or different standards for the outcome. If you understand their values and judgments, you have a better chance of persuading others to act differently or of understanding why they choose what they do.

Let's try it!

A simple example

> A grade school in North Dakota announced it was cancelling recess in the winter months, from November through February. "We have so much snow and such cold temperatures during those months, we can't let the kids outside anyway," said the principal. The school board approved this move, saying the school could use the time to prepare students for tests.

The principal and the superintendent agreed on the decision to cancel recess in the winter. They are looking at the same basic situation.

_____

Identify the basic situation:

_____

Now think about the values behind each person's judgment, based on what each says about cancelling recess. Look at their quotes. Why does the principal judge that cancelling recess is the right decision?

_____

_____

_____

Why does the superintendent judge that cancelling recess is the right decision?

_____

_____

_____

Let's try it!

An example using an actual passage

> The phrase "a wall of separation between church and state" was coined by President Thomas Jefferson in a carefully crafted letter to the Danbury Baptists in 1802, when they had asked him to explain the First Amendment. The Supreme Court, and lower courts, have used Jefferson's phrase repeatedly in major decisions upholding neutrality in matters of religion. . . . Jefferson, explaining the phrase to the Danbury Baptists, said, "the legitimate powers of government reach actions only, and not opinions." Personal religious views are just that: personal. Our government has no right to promulgate religion or to interfere with private beliefs.

Jefferson's phrase about the separation of church and state has been used to make different value judgments about religion.

Why would someone who thinks religion is harmful and has no place in American politics support the decision to keep church and state separate?

_____

_____

Why would someone who thinks religion is valuable and must be protected support the decision to keep church and state separate?

_____

_____

How could the last sentence support both people's beliefs?

_____

_____

Now you try it!

Use one of the articles from the topic on Genetic Engineering (article document numbers EJ3010192215 and EJ3010323209) or choose your own article from the Opposing Viewpoints Resource Center that takes a position on an issue. Find a statement in the article that represents a decision related to the topic. Then explain how different value judgments or standards could lead to this decision. Or, show how different values or standards would lead to different decisions on the topic.

Article Title: _____

Article Document Number: _____

Decision: _____

_____

Value judgments that led to this decision:

1. _____

_____

2. _____

_____

Or

Decision: _____

_____

Value judgments that led to this decision:

1. _____

_____

2. _____

_____

Focus on Critical Thinking Skills

Skill 8

• Examine and investigate ideas in greater detail

Analyzing arguments, interpretations, beliefs, or theories

What does it mean?

> "Look at this!" Aisleen held up the results of the voting in the school election. "Only 44 percent of students voted for class president. What a terrible turnout. It's embarrassing that so few kids voted, especially when both candidates were promising to shorten the school day."
> "Hold on," Josie said. "Forty-four percent of kids voted? That's the highest turnout we've had in years! We usually get 25 percent of kids voting. And considering that no one believed either candidate could really get the school day shortened, this is a great turnout!"

Think about how often you are presented with information to analyze. When people ask your opinion on something, they are asking for you to interpret that information. You interpret information and then use your interpretation to create an argument or a theory.

information   interpretation   argument or theory

The problem is that the same information can be interpreted in different ways. You see that in the student election example above. People's beliefs or prior experience and knowledge can influence their interpretations. If Aisleen believes teens are apathetic and do not care about anything, she will interpret the 44 percent voter turnout as terribly low because it confirms her belief about teens. Notice that Aisleen and Josie also interpret the candidates differently. Aisleen interprets their promise to shorten the school day as exciting, while Josie interprets it as unlikely to succeed.

Why is it important?

Understanding how beliefs and differing perspectives impact interpretations and how one piece of information can generate different interpretations are vital skills. For the rest of your life, you will be asked to interpret information and come up with arguments or theories based on your interpretation. You will have to defend your interpretation and expose flaws in opposing interpretations. You will also need to see the validity in others' perspectives and recognize that although their interpretations of information may differ from yours, they also may be valid. Sometimes two opposing interpretations are both valid.

Let's try it!

A simple example

> "Look at this!" Aisleen held up the results of the voting in the school election. "Only 44 percent of students voted for class president. What a terrible turnout. It's embarrassing that so few kids voted, especially when both candidates were promising to shorten the school day."
> "Hold on," Josie said. "Forty-four percent of kids voted? That's the highest turnout we've had in years! We usually get 25 percent of kids voting. And considering that no one believed either candidate could really get the school day shortened, this is a great turnout!".

What is the information that both Aisleen and Josie interpret?

_____

What extra piece of information does Aisleen introduce?

_____

What extra piece of information does Josie introduce?

_____

To figure out who has the best interpretation of voter turnout, Josie or Aisleen, you have to look at the information yourself. Forty-four percent is less than half—pretty low. But the usual turnout is only 25 percent; compared to that, 44 percent is a big improvement. Another, less concrete, fact is candidate appeal. Each candidate promised to shorten the school day. Was this an exciting reason to vote, as Aisleen believes, or an obvious over-promise, as Josie believes?

Based on the information, including the concrete voter percentage and the less concrete candidate appeal, whose interpretation do you support, Aisleen's or Josie's? Explain the basis for your support for this argument.

_____

_____

_____

_____

Let's try it!

An example using an actual passage

> Of all intervention measures related to demand, price has been shown to be the single most effective means of changing tobacco use behavior. . . . Estimates show that a 10 percent price increase reduces overall young adult consumption by 8 percent, with approximately half of the impact resulting from reductions in the number of young adult smokers; the probability of daily smoking initiation among young adults would decline by about 10 percent.

This author argues that raising the price of cigarettes is the most effective way to reduce youth smoking. This argument is based on the author's interpretation of information. Begin by identifying the information the author interprets. Then think of an opposing interpretation you could make using the same information.

What information is interpreted? Put it in your own words.

_____

_____

_____

What opposing interpretation could you make?

_____

_____

_____

How do you interpret the information differently to come up with this interpretation?

_____

_____

_____

Name _____ **Date** _____

Now you try it!

Use one of the articles from the topic "Narcotics Legalization" (article document numbers EJ3010172259 and EJ3010172260) or choose your own article from the Opposing Viewpoints Resource Center that bases an argument or theory on interpretation of information. Identify the information being interpreted and the argument or theory put forward. Then see if you can use that information to come up with an opposing argument or theory.

Article Title: _____

Article Document Number: _____

Restate the argument and conclusion:

_____

_____

_____

_____

_____

The assumptions are (number them):

_____

_____

_____

_____

_____

_____

_____

Focus on Critical Thinking Skills

Skill 9   Identifying assumptions

• Recognize ideas, beliefs, and theories that are not stated by an author

What does it mean?

> You are sitting around a table with the other members of the drama club at your school. The group is meeting to find ways to raise funds to attend a performance of *Grease*. Carol has been arguing in favor of a bake sale. "There are 500 students at the school," Carol says. "We sell the cookies we make at one dollar per cookie and we'll raise $500. That's more than enough to cover the trip!"

When anyone makes an argument, he or she begins with one or more assumptions. In the example, is Carol making any assumptions? An assumption is a statement, or belief, that is held to be true without a need for proof. Assumptions are the foundations of arguments, but they are typically not considered a part of the argument. Since they are not a part of the facts and evidence presented in an argument, **assumptions are often not stated**. Honest and thoughtful advocates of a position may try to identify all their assumptions, but this is rare. You should also be aware that many assumptions are widely held beliefs that you yourself might hold to be true. For this reason, some assumptions may be difficult for you to see. Indeed, even the person making the argument may not be aware of some of the assumptions he or she is making. Critical thinkers dig for and question assumptions.

Why is it important?

Identifying and questioning assumptions is a key part of critical thinking. It is important to know the assumptions behind an argument, especially when they are not stated. The reason for this is that assumptions are often the key to understanding why an argument might be wrong. If the assumptions behind an argument are wrong, then the conclusion will also likely be wrong.

Let's try it!

A simple example

> You are sitting around a table with the other members of the drama club at your school. The group is meeting to find ways to raise funds to attend a performance of *Grease*. Carol has been arguing in favor of a bake sale. "There are 500 students at the school," Carol says. "We sell the cookies we make at one dollar per cookie and we'll raise $500. That's more than enough to cover the trip!"

What are Carol's unstated assumptions? Begin by identifying Carol's **conclusion;** then state in words a fact or belief (assumption) that Carol has not said out loud that must be true for Carol's conclusion to be true. Finally, consider reasons why the assumptions might be wrong.

Carol's conclusion is: _____

_____

_____

Carol's assumptions are (number them): _____

_____

_____

_____

_____

Let's try it!

An example using an actual passage

> The idea that people should somehow learn to "leave nature alone" has an aura of commendable humility, and it's the easiest thing imaginable to put into words, but it's quite impossible to put into practice in today's world. Proactive environmentalism—which deserves greater support and understanding from progressives—involves managing ecosystems, sometimes in ways that totally transform them. Every ecosystem, every population of wild animals, is, in one way or another, managed by human beings right now.

Assumptions can be more difficult to identify in more complicated arguments. Begin with restating the argument and conclusions. Then write down some assumptions this author is making that might be questioned.

Restate the argument and conclusion: _____

_____

_____

_____

_____

The assumptions are (number them): _____

_____

_____

_____

_____

_____

_____

_____

_____

Now you try it!

Use one of the articles from the topic "Iran" (article document numbers EJ3010238239 and EJ3010238240) or choose your own article from the Opposing Viewpoints Resource Center that takes a position on an issue. Identify two or three assumptions that the author has made in the article in arriving at his or her conclusions.

Article Title: _____

Article Document Number: _____

Restate the argument and conclusion: _____

_____

_____

_____

_____

The assumptions are (number them): _____

_____

_____

_____

_____

_____

_____

_____

Focus on Critical Thinking Skills

Making plausible inferences, predictions, or interpretations

• Provide a reasonable explanation, forecast, or conclusion from information

What does it mean?

> "Great," said Jana angrily. "The star running back for our team just got injured. We're already 10 points behind in the fourth quarter. Without the star, we're bound to lose the game." "I don't think so," said Debjani. "We're on the five-yard line, ready to score. And the quarter just began, so we've got plenty of time to score. Plus, without the star, the rest of the team will play harder. They know they have to step up. We're going to win this game."

We live in a world of forecasts: we try to predict the weather, who will win the big game, what politicians will do, and what the results of those actions will be. It is hard to make **accurate** predictions because we just cannot know what the future holds. But we can make **plausible** predictions. Plausible means "likely," or "believable." A plausible prediction is one that makes sense given the facts we do know, like weather patterns, which team is stronger, and what politicians have done in the past. To make a plausible prediction, or inference, you have to look at the facts as objectively as you can. In the example above, Jana is so anxious for her team to win that she overreacts to the loss of the player. Her fear of losing makes her predict that the team will lose. Debjani, on the other hand, is more objective. She sees the loss of the star as a factor, but she acknowledges that other factors make up for the loss. Her unemotional prediction, or inference, is more credible than Jana's emotional inference.

Why is it important?

Making plausible inferences is a valuable skill because it improves our assessments of the outcomes of actions. Everyone has to make decisions that affect the future. If you can make plausible inferences, you will make better decisions.

Let's try it!

A simple example

> "Great," said Jana angrily. "The star running back for our team just got injured. We're already 10 points behind in the fourth quarter. Without the star, we're bound to lose the game." "I don't think so," said Debjani. "We're on the five-yard line, ready to score. And the quarter just began, so we've got plenty of time to score. Plus, without the star, the rest of the team will play harder. They know they have to step up. We're going to win this game."

Jana's inference: _____

What does Jana base this inference on?

_____

_____

Debjani's inference: _____

What does Debjani base this inference on?

_____

_____

What does Jana infer about the star running back?

_____

_____

What does Debjani infer about the star running back?

_____

_____

Let's try it!

An example using an actual passage

> In a world where women are expected to be sexually available, but also expected to be financially self-supporting, the prevention of childbirth—"reproductive choice"—becomes a necessity. Contraception is a partial solution to this problem, but contraception fails, or participants fail to use it for one reason or another. Thus abortion becomes necessary. . . .

What are the conclusions that this author comes to in this passage? Identify the overall conclusion.

_____

_____

_____

What information does the author use to make these inferences, or conclusions?

_____

_____

_____

_____

What is another plausible inference that could be made from the same information?

_____

_____

_____

_____

_____

Now you try it!

Use one of the articles from the topic "Capital Punishment" (article document numbers EJ3010120257 and EJ3010120258), or choose your own article from the Opposing Viewpoints Resource Center that takes a position on an issue. Identify an important inference in the article, as well as the factors the inference is based on. Then judge whether the inference is plausible.

Article Title: _____

Article Document Number: _____

What is an important inference in the article? _____

_____

_____

What information is that inference based on? _____

_____

_____

Does the author's inference seem plausible? Explain. _____

_____

_____

Provide an alternative inference based on the same information and explain why yours is more or less plausible than the author's inference.

_____

_____

_____

_____

Focus on Critical Thinking Skills

Skill 11   Analyzing or evaluating actions or policies

- Examine the consequence of an undertaking or plan in great detail

What does it mean?

> There is a public meeting tonight with your town council to discuss a new proposed bylaw banning skateboarding and rollerblading on all sidewalks and streets. The action is in response to several complaints by residents that local youth are blocking sidewalks and interfering with pedestrians. You and your friends plan to attend.

Every action has consequences—whether large or small. Banning skateboarding will have several effects on the town. What are they? Decisions and their subsequent actions are undertaken to achieve some goal. In this case, the town council is considering banning skateboarding to protect the rights of its residents. Determining whether a decision or action will accomplish a goal requires an assessment of the possible consequences of the action. **Actions also may have other consequences that may be unforeseen, unpredicted, and possibly unwanted.** Analyzing possible consequences is thus a component of decision-making. Setting aside personal bias in examining consequences is important to being able to generate as many realistic potential consequences as possible. Prior to the implementation of an action, a good grasp of potential consequences also can form part of an argument for or against the action. Once you have analyzed the potential consequences of an action, then you can look for evidence to assist you in determining which of the consequences are the most probable.

Why is it important?

Being able to critically think about many possible consequences of an action is an excellent tool to use in decision-making. In our own lives, we want to make good decisions that have the intended results. Thinking through all the possible consequences is a necessary step in discerning how likely it is that a particular decision will accomplish our goal.

Let's try it!

A simple example

There is a public meeting tonight with your town council to discuss a new proposed bylaw banning skateboarding and rollerblading on all sidewalks and streets. The action is in response to several complaints by residents that local youth are blocking sidewalks and interfering with pedestrians. You and your friends plan to attend.

If the town council bans skateboarding and rollerblading on sidewalks, what will be the consequences? Consider as many different aspects of the action as possible, including its effect on different sorts of town residents, immediate versus long-term effects, and positive and negative effects. In point form, state at least six different possible consequences.

Possible consequences of banning skateboarding and rollerblading on sidewalks:

_____

_____

_____

_____

_____

_____

_____

_____

_____

_____

_____

_____

_____

Let's try it!

An example using an actual passage

> Smoak contends that environmental tobacco smoke (ETS) has significant adverse effects on the health of those who are forced to breathe it. It is especially hazardous to young children, he maintains. . . . Furthermore, Smoak asserts, ETS should be classified as a human carcinogen and eliminated from workplaces and public buildings.

For some actions or policies, analyzing consequences can be more difficult. In the above passage, what might be the consequences of banning ETS from workplaces and public buildings? To begin, write down a list of the different groups of people that may be affected. Add to your list other aspects of society and the physical environment that may be affected. Then ask yourself the possible ways that each may be affected by the action of banning ETS.

What aspects of society, the physical environment, and groups of people may be affected by a ban of ETS from workplaces and public buildings?

_____

_____

_____

In point form, describe six possible consequences of banning ETS from workplaces and public buildings.

_____

_____

_____

_____

_____

_____

Now you try it!

Use one of the articles from the topic "Campaign Finance Reform" (article document numbers EJ3010230221 and EJ3010230222), or choose your own article from the Opposing Viewpoints Resource Center that describes an action being taken. Identify the goal of the action. List the possible consequences of the action. In your opinion, is the goal of the action a possible consequence?

Article Title: _____

Article Document Number: _____

Possible consequences:

_____

_____

_____

_____

_____

Is the goal of the action a possible consequence?

_____

_____

_____

_____

_____

_____

Focus on Critical Thinking Skills

Skill 12

Comparing analogous situations: transferring insights to new contexts

• Recognize the similarity between two events; use knowledge of one event to understand another event

What does it mean?

> You and your cousins are at a major league baseball game. Your favorite team wins and everyone has a great time. Just as you are leaving the stands, your oldest cousin Joe turns to you and says, "Isn't life just like a baseball game?"

Analogies are comparisons between two scenarios. A communicator will compare what he or she is trying to describe to something that is familiar to the audience. This is a tool to enhance the audience's understanding. It works because when our minds recognize the similarities between the "old" and the "new" ideas, we apply our understanding of the "old" idea to fill in our understanding of the "new" idea. An analogy can communicate a wide range of things in very few words. Joe's analogy between the baseball game and life may communicate a lot about Joe's ideas about life. While analogies are very useful tools in communicating ideas, **both communicator and audience must remember that everyone perceives things differently**. Everyone looks at baseball games differently. One person may dislike baseball and, to him or her, Joe's analogy will be a negative statement about life, while a baseball fan may interpret Joe's statement very differently.

Why is it important?

Analogies are excellent communication tools and are used often. It is important that we are able to analyze the similarities between the two scenarios being compared for two reasons. First, we should be able to increase our understanding of the communicator's message. And second, we should be able to critically assess an analogy to determine objectively whether to allow it to affect our opinion. For example, if a politician is using an analogy with emotional implications for the audience to sway voters' opinions, it is important to be able to discern how applicable the analogy is to remain as objective as possible.

Let's try it!

A simple example

> You and your cousins are at a major league baseball game. Your favorite team wins and everyone has a great time. Just as you are leaving the stands, your oldest cousin Joe turns to you and says, "Isn't life just like a baseball game?"

Compare a game of baseball to life, thinking of four similarities and four differences between the two scenarios. Begin by briefly listing some of the elements of a baseball game. It is important to note that answers will differ from person to person because individual perceptions differ from person to person.

Some elements of a baseball game:

_____

_____

_____

Similarities between a baseball game and life:

_____

_____

_____

_____

Differences between a baseball game and life:

_____

_____

_____

_____

Name _____ **Date** _____

Let's try it!

An example using an actual passage

> Children, Quart argues, have been transformed into "victims of the contemporary luxury economy." To her, the villains in this case are obvious: They are the corporations that heartlessly market to underage consumers, slavering after the annual $155 billion in discretionary income Quart says they control (although the source of that figure is not cited). Some of her anecdotal evidence is chilling, such as the 150 school districts nationwide that have accepted soft-drink companies' sponsorships, taking relatively small donations in return for exclusive on-campus access to the districts' thirsty young customers. Quart reports that one young rebel who wore a Pepsi shirt to his school's Coca-Cola Day was suspended for "insurrection."
>
> Still, isn't criticizing a marketer for targeting a group of affluent consumers, whatever their height, equivalent to deploring your cat for targeting songbirds? It's in the nature of the beast. . . .

For complex scenarios or ideas, fully grasping analogies is more difficult. In the above passage, the author compares criticizing marketers for targeting children to criticizing a cat for targeting songbirds. To understand the analogy, list the elements of a cat targeting birds, considering the cat, the bird, and the actions involved. Then list as many similarities and differences between the two scenarios as you can. Note that answers will differ as they reflect the perceptions of individuals.

List some elements of a cat targeting a songbird:

_____

List some similarities between a cat targeting a songbird and a marketer targeting children:

_____

_____

List some differences between a cat targeting a songbird and a marketer targeting children:

_____

_____

_____

Now you try it!

Use one of the articles on the topic "Fast Food Restaurants" (article document numbers EJ3010380222 and EJ3010380223) that makes the comparison between fast food restaurants and tobacco companies; or, choose your own article from the Opposing Viewpoints Resource Center that includes an analogy. List the similarities and differences between the two scenarios. Does the analogy increase your understanding of the author's argument? Do you think the author is using the analogy to sway your opinion? If so, did it affect your opinion?

Article Title: _____

Article Document Number: _____

Elements of the familiar scenario:

_____

_____

Similarities between the scenarios in the analogy:

_____

_____

_____

Differences between the scenarios in the analogy:

_____

_____

_____

Do you think the author is using the analogy to sway your opinion? If so, did it affect your opinion?

_____

_____

Focus on Critical Thinking Skills

Skill 13

Recognizing cause and effect

• Identify how one event makes another event happen.

What does it mean?

You are looking forward to playing field games at your class's spring picnic, which is scheduled for Saturday, with Sunday as the rain date. There is a thunderstorm on Saturday morning, so the picnic is rescheduled for Sunday. On Sunday the weather is warm and sunny. The field is muddy as a result of the storm, but the class still has a great time playing games in the mud!

Real-life situations usually involve several events, ideas, or actions. To understand a situation, it is important not only to know what events have occurred but also to understand how they are related. Cause-effect relationships have two parts: a cause is an event, action, or idea that brings about an effect. In the situation described, which events are causes? Which events are effects? Some words and phrases that signal causes are *because, due to,* and *on account of.* Some words and phrases that signal effects are *so, thus, therefore,* and *as a result.* An event can have more than one cause and more than one effect, and a single event can be both a cause and an effect. It is also important to recognize that unrelated events may occur such that there appears to be a cause-effect relationship between them. It can be important to identify the mechanism of the cause-effect relationship in situations in which events might not be related. This is one of the tasks of science. You can use a diagram to represent the cause-effect relationships in a situation. Critical thinkers seek to recognize and understand cause and effect.

Why is it important?

Recognizing cause and effect is a key part of critical thinking. Complex situations involve many events, which are often related in complex ways. Identifying cause-effect relationships can help you get a clearer understanding of a situation so that you can analyze arguments effectively and make informed decisions. A diagram gives a visual representation that makes it easier to see the "big picture."

Let's try it!

A simple example

> You are looking forward to playing field games at your class's spring picnic, which is scheduled for Saturday, with Sunday as the rain date. There is a thunderstorm on Saturday morning, so the picnic is rescheduled for Sunday. On Sunday the weather is warm and sunny. The field is muddy as a result of the storm, but the class still has a great time playing games in the mud!

What are the causes and effects in the picnic situation? Begin by listing the events involved. For each event, identify its cause(s) and effect(s) as stated in the paragraph. Finally, draw a diagram to show how the events are related.

The events:

_____

_____

_____

_____

Event: _____

Cause(s): _____

_____

Effect(s): _____

_____

Continue for the other events on a separate page if necessary.

DRAW YOUR DIAGRAM ON A SEPARATE PAGE.

Let's try it!

An example using an actual passage

> We believe that the tobacco industry fears the continued erosion of its market in this country and as well, the impact of the EPA [Environmental Protection Agency] report on advertising, marketing, and litigation. . . . Because the EPA report strengthens the data on the adverse health consequences of smoking and broadens the hazard to include the nonsmoking majority of the population, the tobacco industry and its allies will continue to oppose it. . . . The AMA [American Medical Association] strongly supports the EPA, as well as the protection of the public from ETS [environmental tobacco smoke] by regulatory and legislative means.

Cause-effect relationships can be more difficult to identify in more complicated arguments. Begin by listing the events involved in the situation. For each event, identify its cause(s) and effect(s) as stated in the paragraph. Finally, draw a diagram to show how the events are related.

The events:

_____

_____

Event: _____

Cause(s): _____

_____

Effect(s): _____

_____

Continue for the other events on a separate page if necessary.

DRAW YOUR DIAGRAM ON A SEPARATE PAGE.

Now you try it!

Use one of the articles from the topic "Sex Education" (article document numbers EJ3010167246 and EJ3010167247), or choose your own article from the Opposing Viewpoints Resource Center. Identify the cause-effect relationships among the events discussed in the article or a portion of the article.

Begin by listing the events involved in the situation. For each event, identify its cause(s) and effect(s) as stated in the paragraph. Finally, draw a diagram to show how the events are related.

Article Title: _____

Article Document Number: _____

The events:

_____

_____

_____

_____

Event: _____

Cause(s): _____

_____

Effect(s): _____

_____

Continue for the other events on a separate page if necessary.

DRAW YOUR DIAGRAM ON A SEPARATE PAGE.

Skill 14 — Demonstrating reasoned judgment

• Show that an opinion or conclusion is based on evidence and logic.

What does it mean?

> You have just watched your school's team win the state basketball championship and are walking behind some classmates who are discussing the season: Sasha, Marisol, Josh, and Tyrell. Marisol suggests the team's improvement this year was a result of the arrival of a new coach. She knows the point guard, who told her that the coach was very motivational and kept everyone focused. Sasha notes that the team this year was very experienced, with only two rookies and a large proportion of senior students. Tyrell laughs and says that it isn't that your school's team is so much better this season, it is that the other teams are really poor. Josh responds by saying that he lives next door to the star of the team, and the star and a teammate have just received major scholarships to attend good colleges.

When an opinion or conclusion is presented, it is often, **but not always**, backed up with information. Sometimes, the information given as the basis of an opinion is reasonable—that is, it is based on factual, relevant evidence and logic. However, the information used to back up an opinion may be nonfactual, illogical, or irrelevant. Discerning whether an opinion is based on evidence and logic or not is one means by which we can determine whether a conclusion or opinion is objective and should be considered.

Why is it important?

Everyone has opinions, and what others think and say affect what we think. It is important then that we have an objective means of assessing the value of the opinions and conclusions of others, so that we may best formulate our own. Our societal laws and public policies are based on the opinions and conclusions of men and women and those who vote for them. Being able to determine whether logic and factual evidence has led to an opinion is a crucial skill in being able to assess critically the conclusions that follow.

Let's try it!

A simple example

> You have just watched your school's team win the state basketball championship and are walking behind some classmates who are discussing the season: Sasha, Marisol, Josh, and Tyrell. Marisol suggests the team's improvement this year was a result of the arrival of a new coach. She knows the point guard, who told her that the coach was very motivational and kept everyone focused. Sasha notes that the team this year was very experienced, with only two rookies and a large proportion of senior students. Tyrell laughs and says that it isn't that your school's team is so much better this season, it is that the other teams are really poor. Josh responds by saying that he lives next door to the star of the team, and the star and a teammate have just received major scholarships to attend good colleges.

Are the opinions of the friends attending the basketball game regarding their team's success valid? To assess the opinions, you need to assess the evidence and logic that has led to them. Begin by briefly describing the opinion of each friend. Then, write the reason given in the paragraph that has led to the opinion. Finally, determine whether the opinion is based on logic and evidence or not.

What are the opinions of the friends regarding the team's success this year?

Sasha: _____

Marisol: _____

Tyrell: _____

Josh: _____

What are the reasons given for each opinion?

Sasha: _____

Marisol: _____

Tyrell: _____

Josh: _____

Is each opinion is based on logic and evidence or not?

Sasha: _____

Marisol: _____

Tyrell: _____

Josh: _____

Name _____ **Date** _____

Let's try it!

An example using an actual passage

> Statistics attest to the importance of race in American life. Blacks
> comprise 12 percent of the U.S. population but 55 percent of those
> who live in poverty for a long time and 60 percent of those who get
> welfare benefits for a long time. Almost seven eighths of the residents
> in extremely high-poverty neighborhoods are members of minority
> groups. Minorities in cities are much more likely to live in such com-
> munities as whites. In 1990, 14 percent of the black population and
> 9.4 percent of the Hispanic population residing in cities lived in
> extremely poor neighborhoods, compared to just 1 percent of the
> white population. Even when blacks gain the wherewithal to escape
> their racially segregated communities and move to white communities,
> whites leave those communities.

For complex arguments, demonstrating that a conclusion is based on reasoned judgment
can be more difficult. Is the author of the above passage using logic and evidence to back
up his or her conclusion? To begin, identify the conclusion the author is making and
write it down. Then, in point form, briefly list three pieces of evidence or logic on which
the conclusion is based.

The author's conclusion: _____

_____

On what evidence and logic is this conclusion based?

_____

_____

_____

_____

_____

_____

Now you try it!

Using one of the articles on the topic "Afterlife" (article document numbers EJ3010123250 and EJ3010355208) or another article of your choice from the Opposing Viewpoints Resource Center, determine whether the conclusion of the author is based on evidence and logic or not. Begin by stating the conclusion of the author. Then list the evidence and logic on which it is based, if there is evidence and logic present.

Article Title: _____

Article Document Number: _____

The conclusion: _____

_____

Evidence and logic on which the conclusion is based: _____

_____

_____

_____

_____

_____

_____

_____

_____

_____

_____

_____

_____

Focus on Critical Thinking Skills

Identifying alternatives

• List different possible conclusions, courses or action, or beliefs to choose between.

What does it mean?

> "Are you going to vote for class president next week?" asked Paul. "Why should I?" said Stefan. "The two candidates are saying exactly the same things. And worse than that, when's the last time a class president actually changed anything around here?" "You have to vote. It's a part of democracy!" Paul exclaimed. "How can it be a democracy when there's no real choice?" asked Stefan. "It's a democracy because you're voting," said Paul. "If you don't vote they'll eliminate the position."

In a variety of situations we are presented with alternatives and asked to choose among them. These alternatives may be conclusions from arguments, decisions to be made, or beliefs to accept. Often the number of alternatives is limited and the choice may seem simple. An important aspect of critical thinking is the ability to identify other alternatives that can be evaluated against those that are being presented. In some contexts there may not be other practical or worthwhile alternatives available at the time you have to make a choice. However, in most situations thinking about the issue from a different perspective, applying different rules, or using different assumptions will lead you to other alternatives to consider. Sometimes this can make what was a difficult choice between two unpleasant alternatives a simple and easy choice for a third alternative.

Why is it important?

Typically there are more ways of looking at a situation than are being presented to you. In many contexts, you may be presented with only a limited set of alternatives because the source of those alternatives has an interest in limiting your choice. Identifying other alternatives can free you from this trap and allow you to make choices better suited to your own interests. This can have practical value, but it also can simply help you understand something better.

Let's try it!

A simple example

> "Are you going to vote for class president next week?" asked Paul. "Why should I?" said Stefan. "The two candidates are saying exactly the same things. And worse than that, when's the last time a class president actually changed anything around here?" "You have to vote. It's a part of democracy!" Paul exclaimed. "How can it be a democracy when there's no real choice?" asked Stefan. "It's a democracy because you're voting," said Paul. "If you don't vote they'll eliminate the position."

What are the three alternatives Stefan is presented with in this passage?

_____

_____

_____

Suggest which alternative Stefan is leaning toward and why.

_____

_____

_____

Suggest another alternative that Stefan might choose. Explain why it might solve the dilemma Stefan has.

_____

_____

_____

_____

Let's try it!

An example using an actual passage

> The library with which most Americans over the age of thirty grew up was the creation of people like William Fletcher and Arthur Bostwick, who, writing at the turn of the century, encouraged librarians to accept responsibility for the library's moral influence in the community. And this is the heart of the change: today the ALA [American Library Association] resoundingly rejects this responsibility as naive and old-fashioned. Its official statements ridicule and ostracize librarians who do not comply with this rejection and library schools teach the new doctrine. The acceptance of moral responsibility for children in the library is now called "unprofessional"; making a responsible moral judgment about materials purchased for the library is called "elitist," and the librarian who is brave enough to do either is labeled a "censor."

In this passage about children's access to materials in public libraries, what alternatives does the author see for libraries?

_____

_____

_____

_____

Suggest at least two possible alternative solutions to the dilemma presented in the passage.

_____

_____

_____

_____

_____

_____

_____

Critical Thinking Skills

Name _____ **Date** _____

Now you try it!

Choose one of the articles from the topic "Animals Deserve Legal Rights" (article document numbers EJ3010344210 and EJ3010309205), or choose your own article from the Opposing Viewpoints Resource Center that offers alternatives on an issue. Identify the alternatives offered and suggest at least three other alternatives that are not discussed in the article.

Article Title: _____

Article Document Number: _____

What are the alternatives presented by the author in the article?

_____

_____

_____

_____

What are at least three other possible alternatives?

_____

_____

_____

_____

_____

_____

_____

Focus on Critical Thinking Skills

Skill 16 — Exploring implications and consequences

- Identify the possible effects of different courses of action

What does it mean?

> "I won't be wearing leather anymore," said Blanca, "because I don't want any more animals to be killed just for my benefit." "That's a pretty big decision," said Ahmed. "Well, it's an easy one for me to make," said Blanca, "because I love animals. Plus, it won't be very difficult to live without leather." "I hope you've thought this through," replied Ahmed. "This may be bigger than you think."

Like any proposed action that has a range of possible consequences that might result once the action is taken, a statement can have a range of implications. You can discover these implications by asking yourself, "If this statement is true, does that mean X is also true?" An important aspect of critical thinking involves identifying and evaluating all of the possible consequences of an action. Likewise, a critical thinker will fully explore the meaning of a statement by identifying all of its implications. Some of the consequences of an action, or the implications of a statement, will be obvious; others will not be obvious. The consequences and implications that are not obvious are the ones that the critical thinker strives hardest to uncover.

Why is it important?

When we carry out an action without knowing its consequences or make a statement without knowing its implications, we run the risk of unexpected and unpleasant surprises. You typically do and say things with the hope of reaching some outcome for yourself, your family, or your community. Analyzing consequences and implications allows us to best match those outcomes with what we hope to accomplish.

Let's try it!

A simple example

> "I won't be wearing leather anymore," said Blanca, "because I don't want any more animals to be killed just for my benefit." "That's a pretty big decision," said Ahmed. "Well, it's an easy one for me to make," said Blanca, "because I love animals. Plus, it won't be very difficult to live without leather." "I hope you've thought this through," replied Ahmed. "This may be bigger than you think."

Blanca makes a statement in this passage and then describes one of its implications ("I won't be wearing leather anymore."). What is the statement?

_____

_____

What are the other possible implications of Blanca's statement? These implications will be things that Blanca is also likely to find herself thinking about or wanting to do as a result of her statement.

_____

_____

_____

_____

_____

_____

_____

Let's try it!

An example using an actual passage

> Instead of a blanket amnesty, what America needs is to allow hardworking, taxpaying individuals who have been residing in the United States for many years the opportunity to earn permanent residency status—the green card—which ultimately would lead to citizenship.

What is the statement being made here?

_____

_____

What are some of the possible implications of this statement?

_____

_____

_____

What are some possible consequences of taking the action described in the statement?

_____

_____

_____

_____

_____

_____

Now you try it!

Use one of the articles from the topic "Human Rights" (article document numbers EJ3010378212 and EJ3010378213), or choose your own article from the Opposing Viewpoints Resource Center. Choose a statement and identify two or three implications you can draw from it. If the statement suggests a specific action, identify two or three possible consequences of that action.

Article Title: _____

Article Document Number: _____

Statement:

_____

_____

Possible implications:

_____

_____

_____

_____

_____

Possible consequences:

_____

_____

_____

_____

_____

Focus on Critical Thinking Skills

Skill 17   Generating or assessing solutions

• Develop answers
and explanations
for problems

What does it mean?

> You have just left your friends after watching a movie at a downtown cinema at 11:30 at night. You are heading to your car to go home. The car is parked on a quiet, deserted residential street, and as you approach, you accidentally drop your car keys down the drain. The car is locked. You call your parents on your cell, but they do not answer. What do you do?

Problems are a part of everyday life and affect people at every level: individuals, groups, societies, the globe, and future generations. A solution for a problem is a set of parameters, actions, or decisions that answer a question and improve or remove a negative scenario. The first step in solving any problem is to define the problem. What is the desired result of a solution? Then think of solutions that may affect the result. Often, **there may be more than one possible solution to a problem,** and sometimes solutions may not be immediately obvious. Thinking of a problem from many angles can help to generate solutions.

Why is it important?

By definition, solving problems is beneficial. Generating solutions to a problem is the critical first step in reaching a goal. The ability to objectively seek different solutions to a problem prior to evaluating them is an important critical thinking skill with immediate benefits.

Let's try it!

A simple example

> You have just left your friends after watching a movie at a downtown cinema at 11:30 at night. You are heading to your car to go home. The car is parked on a quiet, deserted residential street, and as you approach, you accidentally drop your car keys down the drain. The car is locked. You call your parents on your cell, but they do not answer. What do you do?

In point form, generate at least four possible solutions to the problem of dropping your car keys on a deserted street at night. First, state the desired outcome. Then, look at the problem scenario from as many points of view as possible to arrive at solutions. You may list solutions that will arrive at a desired outcome that may not be as feasible or desirable as others. Once you have generated a list of possible solutions, then you can compare and evaluate them. Note that the solutions will change according to the desired outcome.

The desired outcome: _____

_____

Possible solutions to arrive at that outcome:

_____

_____

_____

_____

_____

_____

_____

Let's try it!

An example using an actual passage

> In 2001 the U.S. Surgeon General issued a report showing that the U.S. was suffering from an epidemic of obesity which annually killed about 300,000 Americans and cost us over $100 billion a year. Since that time Congress has done virtually nothing of consequence to deal with this problem....

For complex problems, generating solutions is more difficult. It is important to identify the desired outcome; there may be more than one possibility. With complex problems, achieving a desired outcome may not be possible with just one solution. It thus becomes important to generate as many potential solutions as possible in order to achieve the desired outcome as closely as possible.

The passage above identifies obesity as a problem in the United States. First, identify a desired outcome. Then, generate as many possible solutions as you can. Remember that this exercise is about generating solutions rather than evaluating their comparative merit, so use your imagination.

The desired outcome: _____

_____

Some possible solutions to the problem that will contribute to the desired outcome:

_____

_____

_____

_____

_____

_____

_____

_____

Now you try it!

Using one of the articles on the topic "Environmental Racism" (article document numbers EJ3010332205 and EJ3010332206) or another article of your choice from the Opposing Viewpoints Resource Center, practice generating solutions to a problem. Begin by stating the desired outcome. Then, list as many solutions, whether they are partial or not, that may contribute to the achievement of the desired outcome. Note that in some of these articles, authors differ in their opinions on the reasons for a problem and its solutions but agree on the existence of the problem.

Article Title: _____

Article Document Number: _____

The desired outcome: _____

_____

_____

Potential solutions:

_____

_____

_____

_____

_____

_____

_____

| Skill 18 | **Drawing and testing conclusions** |

· Reconsider a decision based on an analysis of its effects and consequences

What does it mean?

> You and your buddy Jean are avid rock climbers. Steve is a new student in your grade from out of state who tells you he is an experienced rock climber. In conversation, he seemed to know the terminology of the sport, and you invited him along this weekend. Now you're halfway up a rock face, and Steve is totally panicked. You and Jean have to help him back down and abandon the excursion. Was it a bad decision to take Steve with you?

We make small decisions every day. We also make larger decisions throughout our lives. Our politicians make decisions when they pass laws that can affect our families, our societies, and our globe. Once a decision is put into effect, only then can you be sure of the consequences, as they become reality. Analyzing the consequences of a decision—both positive and negative—allows us to test the decision.

Why is it important?

The consequences of a decision may be negative, positive, or neutral and are likely to be a mixture. Analyzing the consequences is important to be able to assess whether an action or course precipitated by a decision should be continued or changed.

Let's try it!

A simple example

> You and your buddy Jean are avid rock climbers. Steve is a new student in your grade from out of state who tells you he is an experienced rock climber. In conversation, he seemed to know the terminology of the sport, and you invited him along this weekend. Now you're halfway up a rock face, and Steve is totally panicked. You and Jean have to help him back down and abandon the excursion. Was it a bad decision to take Steve with you?

In this example, the decision was to bring Steve along, and its consequences are minor. There are no major injuries and no major economic losses. Nevertheless, there are consequences. To analyze the consequences of a decision, first identify the decision made. Then, identify the positive, negative, and neutral consequences of that decision. You should list in point form a total of at least five consequences.

The decision: _____

_____

_____

Positive consequences: _____

_____

_____

Negative consequences: _____

_____

_____

Neutral consequences: _____

_____

_____

Was it a bad decision? _____

Let's try it!

An example using an actual passage

> Megan's Law, the first amendment to the Jacob Wetterling Crimes Against Children and Sexually Violent Offenders Act, was passed in October 1996. Megan's Law mandated all states to develop notification protocols that allow public access to information about sex offenders in the community. . . .
>
> Washington, which passed a public notification law in 1990, preceding Megan's Law, is the only state that has researched the efficacy of its public notification law. The State of Washington found no reduction in sex crimes against children; however, a benefit was the level of community education regarding sex crimes. As of 2002, there are no other published studies that demonstrate the efficacy of Megan's Law.

For complex problems, analyzing consequences and benefits is more difficult. Was the passage of Megan's Law a good decision in your view? To help you decide, first determine the purpose of the decision. Then, list in point form any positive, neutral, and negative consequences of the law that are described above. Note that two individuals recognizing the same consequences still may differ in their opinions about whether the decision was a good one or not.

Purpose of Megan's Law: _____

Positive consequences: _____

_____

Negative consequences: _____

_____

Neutral consequences: _____

_____

In your view, was Megan's Law a good decision? _____

Now you try it!

Using one of the articles on the topic "Mifepristone" (article document numbers EJ3010102266 and EJ3010102267) or another article of your choice from the Opposing Viewpoints Resource Center, practice evaluating the consequences of a decision. Begin by stating the decision and the desired outcome. Then list as many positive, negative, and neutral consequences as you can. Do you think the decision should remain unchanged or be changed?

Article Title: _____

Article Document Number: _____

The decision: _____

The desired outcome: _____

Positive consequences: _____

_____

_____

Negative consequences: _____

_____

_____

Neutral consequences: _____

_____

_____

In your opinion, should the decision be changed? _____

_____

_____

Skill 1 Evaluating the credibility of information sources

Let's try it!

A simple example—answers, (page 2 exercise)

The sources of the information about *Muscle X* are Tim, Tim's trainer, and the information on the bottle's label.

Depending on the trainer's educational background, he could be an expert on nutrition and physical fitness.

If Tim's trainer is a dealer or spokesman for *Muscle X*, he could make money by selling the product. The information on *Muscle X's* label is intended as an advertisement, and any scientific claims on the label should not be taken at face value.

Without more information, it is hard to judge whether Tim's trainer is a credible source of information. The most credible sources of information about *Muscle X* would be a nutritionist or sports physician.

Skill 1 Evaluating the credibility of information sources

Let's try it!

An example using an actual passage—answers, (page 3 exercise)

The American Medical Association is the source of the information in this paragraph.

The American Medical Association is a credible source for information about public health since the association is composed of doctors and other public health officials.

Whether the American Medical Association could be considered a credible source of information about the media depends on the context of the information. In the context of the paragraph, it is a credible source because the information concerns the connection between the media and public health.

The poll itself is credible, but the opinions of laypeople may not be credible, because laypeople are not experts in the subject area they are discussing and the opinions given may be presented in a way meant to further an individual's own social agenda.

Skill 2 Distinguishing relevant from irrelevant facts

Let's try it!

A simple example—answers, (page 6 exercise)

Gina is researching the causes of the seasons.

The second passage Gina found reads, "When light rays strike the Northern Hemisphere most directly, the season of summer occurs. When light rays strike the Northern Hemisphere at an angle, the season of winter occurs." This passage is relevant to the topic she is researching because it discusses the cause of summer and winter.

The first passage Gina found reads, "As we move around the Sun over the course of the year, we see different parts of the Milky Way galaxy in the night sky. This is why the constellations, or star patterns, seem to change in seasonal cycles." While this is interesting information about constellations, it is irrelevant to the topic Gina is researching because it does not relate to the causes of the seasons.

Skill 2 Distinguishing relevant from irrelevant facts

Let's try it!

An example using an actual passage — answers, (page 7 exercise)

The passage is discussing possible reasons people have for leaving Mexico and immigrating illegally to the United States. The author of the passage also is assigning blame for the situation to the government of Mexico. Both of these lines of thought are relevant to the topic of illegal immigration.

The passage discusses the state of wealth distribution in Mexico rather than in the United States. Therefore, the information in the passage is irrelevant to the topic of poverty in the United States.

Skill 3 Distinguishing fact from opinion

Let's try it!

A simple example—answers, (page 10 exercise)

The park ranger gave Lee the following pieces of factual information:

- ❏ The park contains three different ecosystems
- ❏ The park has some of the most diverse animal life in the country.
- ❏ Certain plants and animals are likely to be seen on each trail.

All of these statements could be proven by objective data.

The park ranger stated the following opinions to Lee:

- ❏ The park is more scenic than other nearby state parks
- ❏ Some of the park's hiking trails are more challenging than others.

None of these statements can be proven with objective data.

Skill 3 Distinguishing fact from opinion

Let's try it!

An example using an actual passage — answers, (page 11 exercise)

Statements of fact given in the passage include:

❏ The restaurant became packed with people.

❏ The restaurant began to receive negative letters and phone calls.

❏ Animal rights activists had heard about Heat's fresh sashimi.

❏ Fish arrived at the table fully alive—with chunks cut out of the belly.

❏ It is a common practice in Japan to serve live fish.

❏ The Bureau of Animal Welfare ordered Heat to stop what it was doing, and the restaurant complied.

❏ Changes in the restaurant's serving practices have not hurt its business.

❏ The restaurant owner lives in the United States.

Statements of opinion given in the passage include:

❏ Reports about the serving practices of the restaurant were everything a restaurateur could ask for.

❏ Chan's arguments fell on deaf—or disgusted—ears.

❏ The restaurant owner has to make everybody happy.

Skill 4 Recognizing contradictions

Let's try it!

A simple example—answers, (page 14 exercise)

The article gives us the following statements:

- ❑ Your town's city council has approved the construction of three new roads around your town.

- ❑ All three of the roads will be tolled.

- ❑ The council came to the decision because tolling drivers on the new roads is the fastest way to pay for their construction.

- ❑ The mayor said that as soon as the construction costs of the new roads were paid for, the tollbooths would be removed.

- ❑ In addition to the tollbooths on the new roads, permanent tollbooths would be added to another local highway that was constructed 10 years ago.

Some of the statements in the article contradict each other. For example, the city council supposedly agreed to toll some roads to pay for the roads' construction. However, a road that has been built already will also be tolled. Also, the mayor says that the tollbooths will be removed when construction costs are paid. However, the tollbooths on the older road are "permanent."

Answer Page

Skill 4 Recognizing contradictions

Let's try it!

An example using an actual passage — answers, (page 15 exercise)

Interpretations of this passage can vary with point of view. However, given the definition of the word *fundamentalism*, you can extrapolate that the term *Islamic fundamentalism* means "rigid adherence to the basic principles of Islam." The author describes Islam by saying, "the teachings of the Koran are infallible and cannot be bent and shaped to fit modern times or fads," "people of the Islamic faith have the right and duty to practice their beliefs as they have for more than thirteen hundred years," and "the tenets of the faith must remain as Muhammad dictated them in the seventh century." Each of these descriptions is consistent with the definition of *fundamentalism* because the statements imply that Muslims must rigidly adhere to their beliefs. Thus, the author contradicts him- or herself when saying that Islamic fundamentalism does not exist.

Skill 5 Recognizing bias

Let's try it!

A simple example—answers, (page 18 exercise)

The manufacturer of the medicine provides the information on the cold-medicine label. It has an interest in selling you the medicine to make money for its company. Thus, any information presented by the manufacturer would most likely be biased.

The pieces of information on medicine labels that you could trust would come from the government or professional associations that allow their names or symbols to be used when a product meets certain standards. In the case of this medicine, you can trust that it is indeed FDA approved.

The claim that you could get rid of your cold in four hours goes against common sense. The medicine might help you recover from the cold in a shorter period of time than usual or relieve symptoms in four hours, but it is extremely unlikely that the medicine can cure the cold in four hours.

For unbiased information about the cold medicine, you could go to your family physician, the pharmacist at the store, or another trained medical professional.

Skill 5 Recognizing bias

Let's try it!

An example using an actual passage — answers, (page 19 exercise)

The author of the passage is anti-abortion. You can understand that the author is taking this stance when the author states that the country is not what it ought to be because abortion is legal and that it is the responsibility of the citizens to protect the weakest among us.

If the author presented statistics about abortion, it is likely the statistics would be biased to paint abortion in a negative light. By presenting the information in such a way, the author would support his or her stance on abortion.

Skill 6 Clarifying issues, conclusions, or beliefs

Let's try it!

A simple example—answers, (page 22 exercise)

Each of the swim meets was preceded by a week in which at least two of the team's members were sick. The fact that these members were sick caused the poor performance at the meets. Increasing practice time might actually make team members more sick and would therefore not be a good solution.

Team members consistently perform more poorly at the meets than they do in practice, suggesting that the real issue is that team members get nervous and freeze up at meets. Increasing practice time would probably not fix this problem since the cause is poor performance under conditions of competition.

Skill 6 Clarifying issues, conclusions, or beliefs

Let's try it!

An example using an actual passage — answers, (page 23 exercise)

The speaker here comes to a conclusion that seems vague at first—"something is wrong." But the statistics he uses tell us that he actually has a clear definition of the issue: youth crime is rising rapidly and alarmingly, reaching incredibly high levels.

He says that during the period from 1985 to 1991, the rate of homicide committed by 13- and 14-year-old boys increased 157 percent, while the rate among 15-year-old boys increased 212 percent.

One way the statistics could be made more clear is to present them as real numbers rather than percent changes. For example, how many homicides did 13- and 14-year-olds commit in 1985 and then in 1991 in the United States? If the numbers were low compared to all homicides, we might find the change less alarming. In addition, it is not clear why 13- and 14-year-olds are combined, while 15-year-olds are separated out. Perhaps there was little change in the 14-year-old group, leading to a less-clear conclusion.

Skill 7 Developing criteria for evaluation: clarifying values and standards

Let's try it!

A simple example—answers, (page 26 exercise)

The basic situation is that the school has time set aside for recess that it cannot always use.

Looking at their quotes, we see that the principal judges that it is not safe or healthy to have the students go outside for recess in the winter. The superintendent makes a different judgment, that recess is a waste of time that could be spent studying.

The superintendent might decide to cancel recess in the warmer months, too. So if you were a student trying to get her to change her mind, you would have to prove that recess was not a waste of time because it actually helps students relieve stress so they can learn more. You could not argue that students need recess just because it is fun or healthy. That would work with the principal but not with the superintendent.

Each person came to the same decision, but when you use his or her quotes to clarify values, you see they based their decisions on very different value judgments.

Skill 7 Developing criteria for evaluation: clarifying values and standards

Let's try it!

An example using an actual passage—answers, (page 27 exercise)

The call for a separation of church and state is a decision—a decision to keep religion out of politics and politics out of religion.

But that decision can be based on different judgments. Someone who thinks that religion is harmful and has no place in American politics would decide to approve of separation of church and state so that religion could not influence politics. This person would see separation as making religion weak and politics strong.

Someone who thinks religion is valuable and must be protected would decide in favor of separation so that politics could not interfere with, or limit the expression of, religious faith. This person would see separation as keeping religion strong and far from politics.

Person A would support the last sentence—"Our government has no right to promulgate religion or to interfere with private beliefs"—because she thinks religion is not a worthy pursuit for government. Person B would also agree with the sentence because she thinks politicians have no right to regulate religion.

Skill 8 Analyzing arguments, interpretations, beliefs, or theories

Let's try it!

A simple example—answers, (page 30 exercise)

Aisleen and Josie both interpret the 44 percent voter turnout.

The piece of information that Aisleen introduces is the candidates' promise to shorten the school day.

The piece of information that Josie introduces is the previous voter turnout (25 percent).

If you support Aisleen's interpretation, you probably believe that the candidates' promise to shorten the school day should have excited students. You probably also believe that 44 percent voter turnout is very low, even if it is higher than usual. You would argue that voter turnout was improved but still poor.

If you support Josie's interpretation, you probably believe that the candidates' promise to shorten the school day was an empty promise and not an incentive to vote. You probably also believe that an improvement in voter turnout of nearly 20 points is impressive, especially since there was no exciting reason for students to vote.

Skill 8 Analyzing arguments, interpretations, beliefs, or theories

Let's try it!

An example using an actual passage — answers, (page 31 exercise)

The information being interpreted is that a 10 percent price increase for cigarettes reduces overall young-adult smoking by 8 percent, with about half of that reduction coming from young adults who quit smoking altogether. If the price of cigarettes is raised by 10 percent, 10 percent fewer young adults would start smoking.

In other words, raise the price of cigarettes by 10 percent, and two things happen: the number of young adult smokers goes down by 8 percent; and the number of young adults who start smoking goes down by 10 percent.

You could interpret this information differently. One way you could interpret it differently would be to argue that cutting the number of young adult smokers by 8 percent is not very much. Just 8 percent? You could argue that raising cigarette prices results in a small decrease in young adult smoking, but other actions, like anti-smoking education or banning smoking, could result in a much greater decrease in young adult smoking.

Skill 9 Identifying assumptions

Let's try it!

A simple example—answers, (page 34 exercise)

Carol's conclusion is that the cookie sale will earn $500.

Carol's assumptions are:

❏ That each student at the school will buy one cookie.

This assumption appears to be behind Carol's argument and conclusion that the outcome of the sale will be $500 earned. One can quickly see what problems there might be with this assumption—why it might be wrong. For example, some students will be absent that day, some may not like cookies, some may not have enough money, and some may choose to spend the money they have in other ways. All of these things make the truth of Carol's assumption questionable.

❏ That there will be 500 cookies made.

This assumption is more under the control of the club since they may be able to make sure that the 500 cookies get made. But this assumption may also be wrong if no one has enough time to make all 500 cookies. They also may not have all the ingredients necessary to make 500 cookies.

Skill 9 Identifying assumptions

Let's try it!

An example using an actual passage—answers, (page 35 exercise)

In this case the author is arguing that we cannot protect nature by "leaving it alone," that we manage all of nature now anyway; therefore, we should protect nature by managing ecosystems. Notice that the conclusion is actually in the middle of this set of statements.

Here are some assumptions this author is making:

The author assumes that all management programs will have the intended positive outcomes—that we can accomplish what we set out to do.

In a related assumption, the author assumes that the outcomes we want for management are just as good as (or better than) the outcomes that would occur without management.

The author assumes that there are only two possible approaches, leaving nature alone (having no impact?) and managing it, or controlling outcomes.

In arguing against this author's position, you could begin by identifying ways the assumptions may be wrong or finding evidence that they are wrong.

Skill 10 Making plausible inferences, predictions, or interpretations

Let's try it!

A simple example—answers, (page 38 exercise)

❑ Jana infers that the team will lose. She bases this inference on the loss of the star running back.

❑ Debjani infers that the team will win. She bases this inference on the team's position on the field, how much time is left in the game, and the team's reaction to the loss of the star running back.

Debjani's inference is more plausible than Jana's because Debjani bases her inference on many factors rather than just one.

❑ By saying that the team will lose without the star running back, Jana infers that he is the most important factor in the whole game.

❑ By saying that the team can recover from the loss, Debjani infers that the star running back is just one factor among many.

Jana lets her nerves get the better of her. She is so anxious for her team to win that she sees a single setback as a deathblow to the team's hopes of victory. This makes her inference less plausible: can one player really be the only important factor in a game?

Skill 10 Making plausible inferences, predictions, or interpretations

Let's try it!

An example using an actual passage—answers, (page 39 exercise)

The author concludes that women's reproductive choice is a necessity and comes to the overall conclusion that abortion is a necessity.

The author concludes that reproductive choice is necessary for the following reasons:

❑ Women are expected to be sexually available.

❑ Women are expected to be financially self-supporting.

The author further concludes that abortion is necessary for the following reasons:

❑ Reproductive choice is necessary.

❑ Contraception (which provides reproductive choice) is unreliable.

Another plausible conclusion might be that more liberal adoption policies are a necessity. There may be other possible answers.

Skill 11 Analyzing or evaluating actions or policies

Let's try it!

A simple example—answers, (page 42 exercise)

Some possible consequences of the town council's banning skateboarding and rollerblading on sidewalks are the following:

❏ Local youth may become upset at what is perceived as a restriction of freedom.

❏ Local youth may rebel against the restriction; perhaps there will be some vandalism.

❏ Town council may work with youth to fulfill their needs, perhaps build a new skateboard park, enhance an existing park, or create a rollerblading trail.

❏ Local residents, such as families with young children and the elderly, will be pleased at what is perceived as increased freedom to use sidewalks.

❏ Risk of youth on rollerblades or skateboards being hit by a car is reduced (assuming the activities are banned on roads).

❏ Risk of damage to public property caused by skateboarding tricks is reduced.

❏ Cost of enforcing the bylaw may be high.

❏ It may be difficult to enforce the bylaw, and the issue may escalate.

❏ It may be difficult to enforce the bylaw, police presence on the streets may increase, and crime rate may drop.

Skill 11 Analyzing or evaluating actions or policies

Let's try it!

An example using an actual passage—answers, (page 43 exercise)

Aspects of society, the physical environment, and groups of people that may be affected by a ban of ETS from workplaces and public buildings are the following:

❑ Smokers

❑ Non-smokers

❑ Business owners

❑ Taxpayers

❑ Buildings and furnishings

Some possible consequences of banning ETS from workplaces and public buildings are the following:

❑ Smokers will smoke outside.

❑ Non-smokers will be exposed to less secondhand smoke in enclosed buildings.

❑ Non-smokers may be exposed to more secondhand smoke outside buildings.

❑ There may be a reduction in the amount of tobacco smoked and/or the number of smokers.

❑ There may be a drop in smoking-related disease, decreased health costs, and therefore decreased taxes.

❑ There may be a drop in tax revenue from the sale of tobacco.

❑ Businesses, such as bars, may lose revenue from smoking clientele.

❑ Some businesses may ignore the new law and pay fines instead.

❑ There may be decreased cost in the maintenance of public buildings, carpets, furnishings, etc., because of less cigarette smoke staining.

Answer Page

Skill 12 Comparing analogous situations: transferring insights to new contexts

Let's try it!

A simple example—answers, (page 46 exercise)

Some elements of a baseball game:

- ❏ Two teams
- ❏ Winners and losers
- ❏ Score is kept
- ❏ Different positions
- ❏ Equipment
- ❏ Innings
- ❏ Taking turn at bat
- ❏ Stealing bases
- ❏ Homerun

Similarities between a baseball game and life:

- ❏ Both have defined stages.
- ❏ Both have people that have different roles within teams.
- ❏ Success depends both on personal actions as well as on the actions of those around you.
- ❏ Both are enjoyable.

Differences between a baseball game and life:

- ❏ There are not defined winners and losers in life.
- ❏ There are no defined rules about taking turns in life.
- ❏ There is no score kept in life.
- ❏ While people work together in life, there are always more than two teams; life is much more complicated.

Answer Page

Skill 12 Comparing analogous situations: transferring insights to new contexts

Let's try it!

An example using an actual passage, (page 47 exercise)

List some elements of a cat targeting a songbird:

- ❏ A cat is a predator.
- ❏ A songbird is prey.
- ❏ Cats and songbirds react with instinct and some learning.
- ❏ Instinct can result in the death of the songbird.
- ❏ Instincts cannot be altered or changed.

List some similarities between a cat targeting a songbird and a marketer targeting children:

- ❏ Children and birds are innocent.
- ❏ Cats' and marketers' actions are at the birds' and children's expense.
- ❏ If a songbird is made available to a cat, the cat will target it; if a child with discretionary income is made available to a marketer, the marketer will target it.
- ❏ Neither cats nor marketers are inherently evil.

List some differences between a cat targeting a songbird and a marketer targeting children:

- ❏ Marketers have conscious choice over their actions; cats do not.
- ❏ Marketers do not need to target children to eat.
- ❏ Marketers' targeting children does not result in the death of the children.
- ❏ Marketers' targeting children can be altered through laws.

Answer Page

Skill 13 Recognizing cause and effect

Let's try it!

A simple example—answers, (page 50 exercise)

The events:

❑ There is a thunderstorm Saturday morning.

❑ The picnic is rescheduled for Sunday.

❑ On Sunday the field is muddy.

❑ The class still has a great time playing games in the mud.

Event: There is a thunderstorm Saturday morning.
Effects:

❑ The picnic is rescheduled for Sunday.

❑ On Sunday the field is muddy.

Event: The picnic is rescheduled for Sunday.
Cause: There is a thunderstorm Saturday morning.

Event: On Sunday the field is muddy.
Cause: There is a thunderstorm Saturday morning.
Effect: The class still has a great time playing games in the mud.

Event: The class still has a great time playing games in the mud.
Cause: On Sunday the field is muddy.

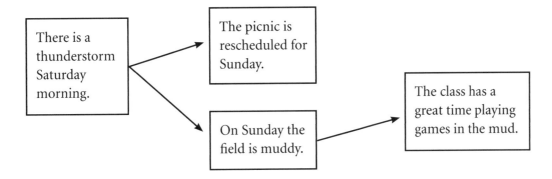

Skill 13 Recognizing cause and effect

Let's try it!

An example using an actual passage—answers, (page 51 exercise)

The events:

- ❏ The tobacco industry fears the impact of the EPA report.
- ❏ The EPA report strengthens data on adverse health consequences of smoking.
- ❏ The tobacco industry and its allies oppose the EPA report.
- ❏ The AMA strongly supports the EPA.

Event: The tobacco industry fears the impact of the EPA report.
Cause(s):

- ❏ The EPA report strengthens data on adverse health consequences of smoking.
- ❏ The AMA strongly supports the EPA.

Effect(s):

- ❏ The tobacco industry and its allies oppose the EPA report.

Event: The EPA report strengthens data on adverse health consequences of smoking.
Effect(s):

- ❏ The tobacco industry and its allies oppose the EPA report.
- ❏ The AMA strongly supports the EPA.
- ❏ The tobacco industry fears the impact of the EPA report.

Event: The tobacco industry and its allies oppose the EPA report.
Cause(s):

- ❏ The tobacco industry fears the impact of the EPA report.

Event: The AMA strongly supports the EPA.
Cause(s):

- ❏ The EPA report strengthens data on adverse health consequences of smoking.

Effect(s):

- ❏ The tobacco industry fears the impact of the EPA report.

The EPA report strengthens data on adverse health consequences of smoking.

The AMA strongly supports the EPA. → The tobacco industry fears the impact of the EPA report. → The tobacco industry and its allies oppose the EPA report.

Skill 14 Demonstrating reasoned judgment

Let's try it!

A simple example—answers, (page 54 exercise)

What are the opinions of the friends regarding the team's success this year?

Sasha: Team has improved.

Marisol: Team has improved.

Tyrell: Team has not improved.

Josh: Team has improved.

What are the reasons given for each opinion?

Sasha: New coach, who is reported by one player to be considered motivational and who helps the team to focus.

Marisol: Team is experienced; only two rookies and a majority of players are seniors.

Tyrell: Other teams are playing badly.

Josh: Team has good players; he has firsthand knowledge of one player with college scholarship, secondhand knowledge of another.

Is the opinion based on logic and evidence or not?

Sasha: Yes, Sasha's opinion is based on logic and evidence.

Marisol: Marisol's opinion is based on logic and evidence.

Tyrell: Tyrell's opinion is not based on logic and evidence.

Josh: Josh's opinion is based on logic and evidence.

Skill 14 Demonstrating reasoned judgment

Let's try it!

An example using an actual passage—answers, (page 55 exercise)

The author's conclusion:

❑ Poverty rates are significantly affected by race in the United States.

On what evidence and logic is this conclusion based?

❑ At 12 percent of the U.S. population, blacks make up 55 percent of those who live in poverty for a long time and 60 percent of those who get welfare benefits for a long time.

❑ Almost seven of eight residents in extremely high-poverty neighborhoods are members of minority groups.

❑ In cities in 1990, 14 percent of the black population and 9.4 percent of the Hispanic population lived in extremely poor neighborhoods versus 1 percent of the white population.

Note that the statement "Even when blacks gain the wherewithal to escape their racially segregated communities and move to white communities, whites leave those communities," while supporting the conclusion, is not backed up with evidence.

Skill 15 Identifying alternatives

Let's try it!

A simple example—answers, (page 58 exercise)

Stefan appears to be presented with the following three alternatives:

❏ Vote for one candidate for class president

❏ Vote for the other candidate for class president

❏ Do not vote for a candidate for class president

Stefan appears to be leaning toward the third alternative because he sees no difference between the candidates and little value to having a class president.

Stefan might have several alternatives to the three he is considering.

❏ If there is time, Stefan himself could run for the position on a different platform.

❏ Stefan could hold a protest at the polling station to draw attention to the deficiencies he sees in the process.

Each of these alternatives would address the essential problem that Stefan sees with the class president election in a way that has the potential to be more effective than simply not voting.

Answer Page

Skill 15 Identifying alternatives

Let's try it!

An example using an actual passage—answers, (page 59 exercise)

Possible alternatives to those presented in the article might be the following:

❑ Have concerned parents accompany children to the library to oversee the reading and loan materials of their children.

❑ Involve the community, for example on an advisory board, in choices about library purchases.

Answer Page

Skill 16 Exploring implications and consequences

Let's try it!

A simple example—answers, (page 62 exercise)

Blanca states that she does not want any more animals to be killed just for her benefit.

Other possible implications of the statement that Blanca has not described and may not be aware of are the following:

❏ She will not want to buy other products made of leather, such as furniture or a diary with a leather binding.

❏ She will have to think about not eating meat since it involves killing animals.

❏ If she considers not eating meat, she will also have to consider modifying her diet in other ways to obtain the correct nutrients.

❏ She will want to avoid buying products that involve animal testing since those animals are killed also.

Answer Page

Skill 16 Exploring implications and consequences

Let's try it!

An example using an actual passage—answers, (page 63 exercise)

The statement being made in the passage is that hardworking, taxpaying individuals present (illegally) for a long time in the country should be given permanent resident status and eventually citizenship.

Some possible implications of the statement in the passage are the following:

❑ Taxpaying individuals would be identified through records.

❑ Missing tax payments in one or more years might be cause for disqualification.

❑ The amount of time spent in the country by an individual could be documented.

Some possible consequences of taking the action suggested in the statement would be the following:

❑ Increases in the standard of living of those people benefiting from the program

❑ Greater temporary expenditures by government to process the large number of applications and investigate them

Skill 17 Generating or assessing solutions

Let's try it!

A simple example—answers, (page 66 exercise)

The desired outcome: to get home safely

Possible solutions to getting home safely:

- ❏ Call a taxi on your cell phone, go home, and go back for the car and the keys tomorrow.

- ❏ Call a tow truck or local 24-hour garage to come and help you get the keys out.

- ❏ Run after your friends to catch up with them and ask them to help you get the keys out or call their parents.

- ❏ Walk to a local garage or convenience store and ask for assistance.

- ❏ See if there is a strong stick anywhere in the vicinity you may use to pry open the grate to retrieve the keys.

- ❏ Go home with one of your friends.

- ❏ Walk home.

Skill 17 Generating or assessing solutions

Let's try it!

An example using an actual passage—answers, (page 67 exercise)

Desired outcome: a significant reduction in obesity in the United States

Some possible solutions to the problem that will contribute to the desired outcome:

❏ Increased exercise for students during school

❏ Increased community programming involving exercise

❏ Incentives for citizens to exercise and eat well

❏ Policies that limit fat content in commercial foods

❏ Education programs for the public about nutrition and exercise

❏ A tax surcharge on non-nutritional foods

❏ Health warnings on packaging of non-nutritional foods

❏ Tax benefits for expenses related to exercising

❏ Medications that prevent or treat obesity before it causes health problems requiring treatment

Answer Page

Skill 18 Drawing and testing conclusions

Let's try it!

A simple example—answers, (page 70 exercise)

The decision: to bring Steve rock climbing

Positive consequences:

❏ Steve feels included in his peer group.

❏ You learned that your interpretation of someone's words may be different from his perception of the meaning of his words.

Negative consequences:

❏ You have to abandon your excursion.

❏ You have to deal with the possibility of Steve's being embarrassed and uncomfortable.

❏ Steve may have been at risk of getting hurt.

Neutral consequences:

❏ No one got hurt.

❏ Steve learned his limitations.

Was it a bad decision? The decision to take Steve was a personal one, and the analysis of it also will be personal, with any judgments depending on your own values. If being kind to someone and making a friend is more important than missing out on a day of climbing, the decision to take Steve was a good one. If the day of climbing is more important to you, the decision to take Steve was a bad one.

Skill 18 Drawing and testing conclusions

Let's try it!

A simple example—answers, (page 71 exercise)

Purpose of Megan's Law: to protect children from sex offenders

Positive consequences:

❑ Community education regarding sex crimes

Negative consequences:

❑ None given in the passage above (Other articles cite examples of damage done to innocent people as a direct consequence of the law.)

Neutral consequences:

❑ No reduction in sex crimes against children

In your view, was Megan's Law a good decision?

Opinions will vary depending on whether the positive consequence of community education is viewed as benefit enough to justify the cost of enforcing a law that may not achieve its goal of reducing sex crimes against children. Other factors may influence opinions as well, such as views on the rights of the sex offenders for privacy and the general public for information.

Notes

Notes

Notes

Notes